Made in the USA
Las Vegas, NV
26 March 2022

46336910R10056